A chocolate CHRISTMAS

Amy Robertson

BARBOUR
PUBLISHING

ISBN 1-59310-876-1

Scripture quotations are taken from the King James Version of the Bible.

Cover image © Getty Images/Food Pix

Published by Barbour Publishing, Inc., P.O. Box 719, Uhrichsville, Ohio 44683, www.barbourbooks.com

Our mission is to publish and distribute inspirational products offering exceptional value and biblical encouragement to the masses.

Member of the
Evangelical Christian
Publishers Association

Printed in Canada.
5 4 3 2 1

CONTENTS

$\mathcal{T}$here are four basic food groups—milk chocolate, dark chocolate, white chocolate, and chocolate truffles.

UNKNOWN

If you're big on chocolate, chocolate, and *more chocolate*, then you'll adore the recipes in this little book. From traditional chocolate recipes to new twists on old favorites, you'll find something "chocolate-y" to delight your sweet tooth this holiday season.

Cookies and Bars

For unto you is born this day
in the city of David a Saviour,
which is Christ the Lord.

LUKE 2:11

I will honor Christmas in my heart,
and try to keep it all the year.

CHARLES DICKENS

Chewy Chocolate Chunk Cookies

½ cup butter, softened
½ cup chocolate syrup
½ cup sugar
1 cup brown sugar, packed
2 eggs
2 tablespoons corn syrup

2 teaspoons vanilla extract
2½ cups flour
1 teaspoon baking soda
½ teaspoon salt
1 (11.5 ounce) package semisweet
   chocolate chunks

Preheat oven to 375 degrees. In a large bowl, cream together butter, chocolate syrup, sugar, and brown sugar until smooth. Beat in the eggs. Stir in corn syrup and vanilla. In a medium bowl, combine the flour, baking soda, and salt; stir into the creamed mixture until blended. Mix in the chocolate chunks. Drop cookies by spoonfuls onto ungreased cookie sheets. Bake for 12 to 14 minutes in the preheated oven. Allow cookies to cool on baking sheet for 5 minutes before removing to a wire rack to cool completely.

Chocolate Chip Cake Cookies

1 cup butter
1½ cups sugar
2 eggs
1 teaspoon vanilla extract
2 cups flour
½ teaspoon baking soda
½ teaspoon salt
1 cup unsweetened cocoa powder
1 cup walnuts, chopped
1½ cups semisweet chocolate chips

Preheat oven to 350 degrees. In a large bowl, cream together the butter and sugar until light and fluffy. Add the eggs and vanilla and mix thoroughly. In a 1 gallon plastic storage bag, add the flour, baking soda, salt, and cocoa powder. Seal the bag and massage until the ingredients are thoroughly combined. Add the flour and cocoa mixture to the butter and sugar. Stir until the dough appears completely combined. Add the walnuts and chocolate chips; stir well. Drop by teaspoonfuls onto an ungreased cookie sheet. Bake for 10 to 12 minutes. Allow to cool for one minute before removing to a cooling rack to cool completely.

Cherry Chocolate Drop Cookies

1 cup powdered sugar
1 cup butter
2 teaspoons maraschino cherry juice
½ teaspoon almond extract
4 drops red food coloring

2¼ cups flour
½ teaspoon salt
½ cup maraschino cherries,
    chopped and drained
48 milk chocolate drop candies

Preheat oven to 350 degrees. In a large bowl, combine powdered sugar, butter, cherry juice, almond extract, and food coloring; stir until well blended. Add the flour and salt; mix well. Stir in the cherries. Shape the dough into 1 inch balls. Place 2 inches apart on ungreased baking sheets. Bake for 8 to 10 minutes. Remove from oven and immediately top each cookie with a chocolate drop candy, pressing down firmly. Allow to cool completely.

Chocolate Peanut Butter Chip Cookies

2¼ cups flour
1 teaspoon baking soda
1 cup butter, softened
¼ cup sugar
¾ cup light brown sugar, packed

1 teaspoon vanilla extract
1 (3.5 ounce) package instant
    chocolate pudding mix
2 eggs
2 cups peanut butter chips

Preheat oven to 375 degrees. In a small bowl, combine flour and baking soda; set aside. In a large bowl, combine butter, sugar, brown sugar, vanilla, and pudding mix; stir until smooth. Beat in eggs. Stir the flour mixture into the butter mixture. Stir in the peanut butter chips. Drop by heaping teaspoonfuls 2 inches apart onto ungreased baking sheets. Bake for 8 to 9 minutes.

Peanut Chocolate Cookies

2 (2 ounce) semisweet baking
   chocolate bars, broken into pieces
1 cups flour
¾ teaspoon baking soda
½ teaspoon salt
½ cup butter, softened

½ cup brown sugar, packed
¼ cup sugar
2 teaspoons vanilla extract
1 egg
1¼ cups honey-roasted peanuts,
   chopped

Preheat oven to 375 degrees. In a small, microwave-safe bowl, microwave semi-sweet baking chocolate bars on high for 60 seconds; stir. Microwave at additional 10 to 20 second intervals, stirring until smooth. Allow to cool. In a small mixing bowl, combine flour, baking soda, and salt. In a large bowl, beat butter, brown sugar, sugar, and vanilla extract. Add the melted chocolate and egg; stir well. Gradually beat in flour mixture. Fold in the peanuts. Drop by rounded teaspoonfuls onto an ungreased cookie sheet. Bake for 8 to 9 minutes or until edges are set. Allow to cool for 3 minutes before removing to a wire rack to cool completely.

Chocolate Chip Cream Cheese Cookies

4 egg yolks
2 cups butter (do not substitute)
2 cups sugar
2 (8 ounce) packages cream cheese

2 tablespoons almond extract
4 cups flour
Pinch of salt
2 cups chocolate chips

Preheat oven to 375 degrees. Combine egg yolks, butter, and sugar. Add cream cheese and almond extract. Combine flour and salt and add to butter mixture. Add chocolate chips. Drop by spoonfuls onto cookie sheets and bake at 375 degrees until edges turn light brown, approximately 10 minutes.

Chocolate Pudding Cookies

2¼ cups flour
1 teaspoon baking soda
1 cup butter, softened
¼ cup sugar
¾ cup brown sugar, packed
1 teaspoon vanilla extract

1 (4 ounce) package instant
    chocolate pudding
2 eggs
1 (12 ounce) package semisweet
    chocolate chips

Preheat oven to 375 degrees. In a medium bowl, mix flour and baking soda; set aside. In a large bowl, combine butter, sugar, brown sugar, pudding mix, and vanilla extract; beat until smooth. Add the eggs. Gradually add flour mixture. Stir in the semisweet chocolate chips. Drop by rounded teaspoonfuls 2 inches apart onto an ungreased cookie sheet. Bake for 8 to 10 minutes. Allow to cool for 2 minutes before removing to a wire rack to cool completely.

German Chocolate Cookies

1 (18.25 ounce) package
   German Chocolate
   cake mix
2 eggs
½ cup margarine, melted

½ cup quick-cooking oats
1 cup semisweet chocolate
   chips
½ cup raisins

Preheat oven to 350 degrees. In a large bowl, combine cake mix, eggs, margarine, and oats; mix well. Stir in the chocolate chips and raisins. Drop by heaping teaspoonfuls 2 inches apart onto an ungreased cookie sheet. Bake for 9 to 11 minutes or until set. Allow to cool for 2 minutes before removing to a wire rack to cool completely.

Giant Chocolate Chip Cookie

1 cup butter, softened
¾ cup sugar
¾ cup brown sugar, packed
1 teaspoon vanilla extract
2 eggs

2¼ cups flour
1 teaspoon salt
1 teaspoon baking soda
2 cups semisweet chocolate chips
1 cup walnuts, chopped

Preheat oven to 375 degrees. In a large bowl, beat butter, sugar, brown sugar, and vanilla until light and fluffy. Add eggs; beat well. Gradually add the flour, salt, and baking soda; stir until well blended. Stir in chocolate chips and nuts. Spread onto a greased 14 inch round pizza pan. Bake for 20 to 25 minutes. Allow to cool completely. Decorate as desired.

Chocolate Chip Thumbprint Cookies

½ cup brown sugar, packed
½ cup butter, softened
1 teaspoon vanilla extract
½ teaspoon salt
1½ cups flour

¼ cup mini semisweet chocolate
   chips
¼ cup milk
Powdered sugar
1 (16 ounce) can chocolate frosting

Preheat oven to 375 degrees. In a large bowl, combine brown sugar, butter, vanilla extract, and salt. Beat at medium speed with an electric mixer for 2 minutes. Reduce speed to low and add flour, chocolate chips, and milk. Beat until well mixed. Shape dough into 1 inch balls. Place 1 inch apart on ungreased cookie sheets. Make indentation in the center of each cookie with thumb. Bake for 10 to 12 minutes or until lightly browned. Allow to cool completely. Sprinkle cookies with powdered sugar. Spoon about 1 teaspoon of chocolate frosting into the center of each cookie indentation.

Chocolate Chip Cutouts

1 (18 ounce) package refrigerated
chocolate chip cookie dough,
divided
¾ cup sugar

1 (8 ounce) package cream cheese,
softened
1 egg

Preheat oven to 350 degrees. Spread half of the cookie dough into a greased 8x8 inch square baking dish. In a medium bowl, mix cream cheese, egg, and sugar until smooth; spread mixture over the cookie dough in pan. Roll out remaining cookie dough and place over cream cheese mixture. Bake for 35 to 45 minutes or until golden. Allow to cool. Refrigerate for 1 hour; cut into shapes with cookie cutters.

White Chocolate Chip Cookies

1 cup butter, softened
2 cups sugar
2 eggs
2 teaspoons vanilla extract
2 cups flour

¾ cup unsweetened cocoa powder
1 teaspoon baking soda
½ teaspoon salt
1⅔ cups white chocolate chips

Preheat oven to 350 degrees. In a large bowl, cream together the butter and sugar until smooth. Beat in the eggs one at a time, then stir in the vanilla. Combine the flour, cocoa, baking soda, and salt; stir into the creamed mixture. Fold in the white chocolate chips. Drop by rounded teaspoonfuls onto ungreased cookie sheets. Bake for 8 to 10 minutes. Allow cookies to cool on baking sheet for 5 minutes before removing to a wire rack to cool completely.

Chocolate Chip Pudding Cookies

2¼ cups flour
1 teaspoon baking soda
1 cup margarine, softened
¼ cup sugar
¾ cup light brown sugar, packed

1 teaspoon vanilla extract
1 (3.5 ounce) package instant
  vanilla pudding mix
2 eggs
2 cups semisweet chocolate chips

Preheat oven to 350 degrees. In a medium bowl, combine flour and baking soda; set aside. In a large bowl, combine margarine, sugar, brown sugar, vanilla, and pudding mix. Beat until smooth and creamy. Beat in eggs. Gradually stir in flour mixture. Stir in the chocolate chips. Drop dough by heaping teaspoonfuls, about 2 inches apart, onto an ungreased cookie sheet. Bake for 9 minutes or until slightly browned.

Chocolate Cherry Crispies

¼ cup butter, softened
1 cup powdered sugar
1 cup peanut butter
¼ cup and 2 tablespoons mini
   semisweet chocolate chips

¼ cup pecans, chopped
1½ cups crisp rice cereal
½ cup maraschino cherries,
   drained, dried, and chopped
1½ cups flaked, sweetened coconut

In a large bowl, combine butter, powdered sugar, and peanut butter; mix well. Stir in chocolate chips, pecans, cereal, and cherries. Shape dough into 1 inch balls. Roll each ball in coconut. Place on cookie sheets. Refrigerate for 1 hour. Keep refrigerated.

Chocolate Chip Kiss Cookies

1 cup butter, softened
⅓ cup sugar
⅓ cup brown sugar, packed
1 teaspoon vanilla extract

2 cups flour
1 cup mini semisweet chocolate
  chips
48 milk chocolate candy kisses,
  unwrapped

Preheat oven to 375 degrees. In a large bowl, beat butter, sugar, brown sugar, and vanilla until well blended. Add flour; blend until smooth. Stir in chocolate chips. Shape dough around each chocolate kiss candy piece, covering completely. Shape into balls; place on an ungreased cookie sheet. Bake for 10 to 12 minutes or until set. Allow to cool slightly before removing to a wire rack to cool completely.

Chocolate Snappers

1 cup sugar
¾ cup shortening
1 egg
¼ cup corn syrup
2 ounces unsweetened chocolate,
    melted

1¾ cups flour
2 teaspoons baking soda
1 teaspoon cinnamon
¼ teaspoon salt
Sugar

Preheat oven to 350 degrees. In a large bowl, cream together sugar and shortening; add the egg. Blend in corn syrup and chocolate; add flour, baking soda, cinnamon, and salt. Mix until well blended. Shape dough by teaspoonfuls into walnut-sized balls; roll balls in sugar. Place on ungreased baking sheets and bake for 10 to 12 minutes.

Chocolate Pizza Cookies

1 cup butter, softened
¾ cup sugar
¾ cup brown sugar, packed
1 (8 ounce) package cream cheese, softened
1 teaspoon vanilla extract
2 eggs

2¼ cups flour
½ teaspoon baking soda
1 teaspoon salt
1 (12 ounce) package semisweet chocolate chips
¾ cup walnuts, chopped

Preheat oven to 375 degrees. Grease two 12 inch pizza pans; set aside. In a large bowl, beat butter, sugar, brown sugar, cream cheese, and vanilla extract. Add eggs; beat well. In a small bowl, combine flour, baking soda, and salt. Pour the flour mixture into the cream cheese mixture; stir until well blended. Fold in the chocolate chips and walnuts. Divide dough evenly and press into prepared pans. Bake for 20 to 25 minutes or until edges are lightly browned. Cool completely in pans. Cut into pizza slices to serve.

Chocolate Chip Twinkle Cookies

1 cup butter, softened
¾ cup powdered sugar
1 egg yolk, beaten
1 teaspoon vanilla extract
1¼ cups flour

¾ cup cornstarch
⅛ teaspoon salt
1 cup flaked coconut
1 cup semisweet chocolate chips
Sugar

Preheat oven to 375 degrees. In a large bowl, cream the butter. Slowly add in the powdered sugar. Beat in the egg yolk and vanilla; set aside. In a medium bowl, combine flour, cornstarch, and salt. Slowly add flour mixture to the butter mixture; blend well. Stir in the coconut and chocolate chips. Shape into 1 inch balls and place on ungreased cookie sheets. Slightly flatten with the bottom of a glass that has been dipped in sugar. Bake for 10 to 12 minutes.

Orange Chocolate Drop Cookies

¼ cup butter, softened
¾ cup brown sugar, packed
1 egg
1 tablespoon orange zest

1 tablespoon orange juice
1½ cups buttermilk baking mix
½ cup walnuts, chopped
1 cup semisweet chocolate chips

Preheat oven to 375 degrees. In a medium bowl, beat butter. Gradually add the brown sugar; beat until light and fluffy. Add the egg, orange zest, and orange juice; mix until smooth. Add baking mix; mix well. Stir in the walnuts and chocolate chips. Drop by teaspoonfuls onto ungreased cookie sheets. Bake for 10 to 12 minutes. Remove from cookie sheet to wire rack.

Chocolate Oatmeal Cookies

1¼ cups flour
½ teaspoon baking powder
½ teaspoon baking soda
½ teaspoon cinnamon
¼ teaspoon salt
¾ cup butter, softened
¾ cup brown sugar, packed
½ cup sugar

1½ teaspoons vanilla extract
1 egg
2 tablespoons milk
1 (11.5 ounce) package milk
   chocolate chips
1 cup quick-cooking oats
½ cup raisins

Preheat oven to 375 degrees. In a small bowl, combine flour, baking powder, baking soda, cinnamon, and salt. In a large bowl, beat butter, brown sugar, sugar, and vanilla extract until creamy. Beat in the egg. Add the flour mixture to the butter mixture; mix well. Add the milk. Stir in the chocolate chips, oats, and raisins. Drop by rounded teaspoonfuls onto an ungreased cookie sheet. Bake for 10 to 14 minutes or until edges are crisp. Let cool for 3 minutes before transferring to a wire rack to cool completely.

Chocolate Sugar Cookies

¾ cup shortening
1 cup sugar
1 egg
2 (1 ounce) squares unsweetened
   chocolate, melted

¼ cup light corn syrup
2 cups flour
¼ teaspoon baking soda
1 teaspoon ground cinnamon

Preheat oven to 350 degrees. In a large bowl, cream together shortening, sugar, and egg. Stir in melted chocolate and corn syrup. In a small bowl, combine flour, salt, baking soda, and cinnamon. Add flour mixture to chocolate mixture. Chill in refrigerator for 1 hour. Roll dough ⅛ inch thick on a well-floured surface. Cut into shapes with cookie cutters. Bake on an ungreased cookie sheet for 10 to 12 minutes.

Christmas Fudge Cookies

2 cups flour
½ cup baking cocoa
½ teaspoon baking soda
¼ teaspoon salt
¼ cup shortening
½ cup sugar

1 egg
½ cup buttermilk
½ cup molasses
1 teaspoon vanilla extract
¾ cup walnuts, chopped

Preheat oven to 350 degrees. In a medium bowl, combine flour, cocoa, baking soda, and salt; set aside. In a large bowl, cream together the shortening and sugar. Beat in the egg, buttermilk, and molasses; stir in vanilla. Gradually blend in the flour mixture; fold in walnuts. Drop by tablespoonfuls 1½ inches apart onto lightly greased baking sheets. Bake for 12 to 14 minutes or until firm.

Cow Pie Cookies

2 cups milk chocolate chips
1 tablespoon shortening

½ cup raisins
½ cup almonds, chopped

Using a double boiler, melt chocolate chips and shortening. Stir until smooth. Remove from heat; stir in raisins and almonds. Drop by tablespoonfuls onto waxed paper. Chill until ready to serve.

Key Lime
White Chocolate Chipper Cookies

½ cup butter, softened
1 cup sugar
1 egg
1 egg yolk
1½ cups flour

1 teaspoon baking powder
½ teaspoon salt
¼ cup lime juice
1½ teaspoons lime zest
¾ cup white chocolate chips

Preheat oven to 350 degrees. In a large bowl, cream together butter, sugar, egg, and egg yolk. Blend in the flour, baking powder, salt, lime juice, and lime zest. Fold in chocolate chips. Roll dough into walnut-sized balls. Place on ungreased baking sheets and bake for 8 to 10 minutes.

Chocolate Cinnamon Bars

2 cups flour
1 teaspoon baking powder
1½ cups sugar, divided
1 tablespoon and 1 teaspoon
    cinnamon, divided
½ cup butter, softened

½ cup shortening
1 egg, beaten
1 egg, separated
1 cup semisweet chocolate chips
½ cup pecans, chopped

Preheat oven to 350 degrees. Lightly grease a 10x15 inch jelly roll pan; set aside. In a large bowl, combine flour, baking powder, 1 cup sugar, and 1 tablespoon cinnamon. Add the butter, shortening, beaten egg, and egg yolk; mix well. Press into prepared pan. Beat egg white slightly; brush over mixture in pan. In a small bowl combine ½ cup sugar, 1 teaspoon cinnamon, chocolate chips, and pecans. Sprinkle mixture over top. Bake for 25 minutes. Allow to cool completely before cutting into bars.

Chocolate Macaroons

1 (18.25 ounce) package chocolate
   cake mix
⅓ cup butter, softened
2 eggs, divided
1 (14 ounce) can sweetened
   condensed milk

1 teaspoon vanilla extract
1 (12 ounce) package semisweet
   chocolate chips
1⅓ cups flaked, sweetened
   coconut, divided
½ cup walnuts, chopped

Preheat oven to 350 degrees. In a large bowl, combine cake mix, butter, and 1
egg until mixture is crumbly. Press firmly into a greased 9x13 inch baking pan.
In a medium bowl, combine condensed milk, 1 egg, and vanilla extract; stir in
the chocolate chips, 1 cup coconut, and walnuts. Spread over mixture in baking
pan. Top with the remaining coconut. Bake for 30 to 40 minutes or until golden
brown. Cool completely in pan before cutting into bars.

Rainbow Brownies

1 cup margarine, softened
1½ cups brown sugar, packed
1 egg, beaten
1 teaspoon vanilla extract
2 cups flour

½ teaspoon baking soda
1½ cups candy-coated chocolate
   pieces
1 cup walnuts, chopped

Preheat oven to 375 degrees. In a large bowl, cream together margarine and brown sugar until light and fluffy. Add egg and vanilla extract. In a medium bowl, combine flour and baking soda. Add flour mixture to the brown sugar mixture; blend well. Stir in the candy pieces and nuts. Spread the dough into a 9x13 inch baking pan. Bake for 30 to 35 minutes or until the center is set. Allow to cool completely before cutting into bars.

Cocoa Coconut Brownies

½ cup butter or margarine,
   melted
1 cup sugar
1 teaspoon vanilla extract
2 eggs

½ cup flour
⅓ cup baking cocoa
¼ teaspoon baking powder
¼ teaspoon salt
¾ cup sweetened coconut flakes

Preheat oven to 350 degrees. In a medium bowl, stir together butter, sugar, and vanilla. Add eggs; beat well. In another bowl, stir together flour, cocoa, baking powder, and salt; gradually add to egg mixture, beating until well blended. Stir in coconut. Spread batter evenly into a greased 8 inch square baking pan. Bake for 25 to 30 minutes or until brownies begin to pull away from sides of pan. Allow to cool for 3 minutes in pan before transferring to a wire rack to cool completely.

Chocolate Banana Cookie Bars

1 (18 ounce) tube refrigerated
   chocolate chip cookie dough
1 (16 ounce) can chocolate frosting

2 bananas, cut into slices
½ cup walnuts, chopped

Roll out cookie dough onto an ungreased pizza pan; bake according to package directions. Remove from oven. Allow to cool completely. Frost cookie with chocolate frosting. Place the banana slices evenly over the frosting. Sprinkle with walnuts before cutting into bars.

White Chocolate Squares

1 (12 ounce) package white
chocolate chips, divided
¼ cup butter or margarine
1 cup flour
½ teaspoon baking powder
1 teaspoon vanilla extract

1 (14 ounce) can sweetened
condensed milk
1 cup pecans or walnuts, chopped
1 large egg
Powdered sugar

Preheat oven to 350 degrees. Grease a 9x13 inch baking pan. In large saucepan over low heat, melt 1 cup white chocolate chips and butter. Stir in flour and baking powder until blended. Stir in vanilla, sweetened condensed milk, pecans, egg, and remaining chips. Spoon mixture into prepared pan. Bake 20 to 25 minutes. Cool. Sprinkle with powdered sugar; cut into squares. Store covered at room temperature.

Chocolate Mint Bars

1 cup semisweet chocolate chips
1 (14 ounce) can sweetened
    condensed milk
2 tablespoons and ¾ cup butter,
    divided
½ teaspoon peppermint extract
1¼ cups brown sugar, packed

1 egg
1½ cups flour
1½ cups quick-cooking oats
⅔ cup walnuts, chopped
⅓ cup hard peppermint candies,
    crushed

Preheat oven to 350 degrees. In a heavy saucepan over low heat, melt chocolate chips, sweetened condensed milk, and 2 tablespoons butter; remove from heat. Add peppermint extract; set aside. In a large bowl, beat remaining butter and brown sugar until fluffy; mix in egg. Add flour and oats; mix well. Press ⅔ of the oat mixture into a greased 10x15 inch baking pan; spread chocolate mixture evenly over the top. Add nuts to the remaining oat mixture; crumble evenly over chocolate. Sprinkle with peppermint candies. Bake for 15 to 18 minutes or until edges are lightly browned. Allow to cool completely before cutting into bars.

Chocolate Oatmeal Bars

1 cup flour
½ teaspoon cinnamon
1 cup butter, softened
½ cup sugar
½ cup brown sugar, packed
1½ teaspoons vanilla extract

1 egg
1¼ cups quick-cooking oats
1 (11.5 ounce) package milk
    chocolate chips, divided
1 cup walnuts, chopped and divided

Preheat oven to 350 degrees. In a small bowl, combine flour and cinnamon. In a large bowl, beat butter, sugar, brown sugar, and vanilla extract until creamy; beat in egg. Gradually add the flour mixture to the butter mixture. Stir in the oats, ¾ cup chocolate chips, and ½ cup walnuts. Spread into a greased 9x13 inch baking pan. Bake for 22 to 28 minutes or until center is set. Immediately sprinkle with remaining chips; let stand for 5 minutes or until chips are shiny. Sprinkle with the remaining nuts. Allow to cool completely before cutting into bars.

Chocolate Banana Bars

2 cups flour
2 teaspoons baking powder
½ teaspoon salt
¾ cup butter, softened
⅔ cup sugar
⅔ cup brown sugar, packed

1½ teaspoons vanilla extract
2 bananas, mashed
1 egg
1 (12 ounce) package semisweet
    mini chocolate chips
Powdered sugar

Preheat oven to 350 degrees. In a medium bowl, combine flour, baking powder, and salt. In a large bowl, beat butter, sugar, brown sugar, and vanilla until creamy. Beat in bananas and egg. Slowly beat in flour mixture. Fold in the chocolate chips. Spread into a greased 10x15 inch jelly roll pan. Bake for 20 to 30 minutes or until a toothpick inserted in the center comes out clean. Cut into bars and sprinkle with powdered sugar.

Chocolate Caramel Brownies

4 (1 ounce) squares unsweetened
   baking chocolate
¾ cup butter
2 cups sugar
4 eggs

1 cup flour
1 cup pecans, chopped
1 (14 ounce) package caramels
2 tablespoons milk
1½ cups semisweet chocolate
   chunks

Preheat oven to 350 degrees. In a large microwave-safe bowl, microwave chocolate squares and butter on HIGH for 2 minutes or until butter is melted. Stir until chocolate is completely melted. Add sugar and stir until well blended. Beat in the eggs. Add the flour and mix well. Stir in the pecans. Pour into a 9x13 inch baking pan lined with greased foil. Bake for 30 to 35 minutes or until a toothpick inserted in center comes out with fudgy crumbs. Do not overbake. Meanwhile, in a microwave-safe bowl, microwave caramels and milk on HIGH for 2½ minutes, stirring after 1 minute. Stir until caramels are completely melted and mixture is well blended. Gently spread over baked brownie; sprinkle with chocolate chunks. Allow to cool before cutting into bars.

And suddenly there was with the angel
a multitude of the heavenly host praising God,
and saying, Glory to God in the highest,
and on earth peace, good will toward men.

LUKE 2:13–14

Cakes and Pies

O little town of Bethlehem,
how still we see thee lie!
Above thy deep and dreamless sleep
the silent stars go by.
Yet in thy dark streets shineth
the everlasting Light;
The hopes and fears of all the years
are met in thee tonight.

PHILLIPS BROOKS

Chocolate Chip Dream Cake

2 (3.9 ounce) packages instant chocolate pudding mix
1 (18.5 ounce) package chocolate cake mix
2 eggs
2½ cups semisweet chocolate chips

Preheat oven to 350 degrees. Lightly grease a 9x13 inch cake pan. Make chocolate pudding according to package directions. Combine chocolate cake mix, chocolate pudding, and eggs; beat for 2 minutes with an electric mixer on medium speed. Pour batter into the prepared pan. Cover the top with the semi-sweet chocolate chips. Bake for 30 to 35 minutes.

Cherry Fudge Cake

1 (18 ounce) package fudge cake mix   1 teaspoon almond extract
1 (21 ounce) can cherry pie filling   1 (16 ounce) can chocolate frosting
2 eggs, beaten

Preheat oven to 350 degrees. Grease and flour a 9x13 inch baking pan; set aside.
In a large bowl, combine cake mix, pie filling, eggs, and almond extract. Mix
until well blended. Pour mixture into prepared pan. Bake for 40 minutes or until
a toothpick inserted in the center comes out clean. Allow to cool completely
before frosting.

Chocolate Pistachio Cake

1 (18 ounce) package white cake
   mix
1 (3.4 ounce) package instant
   pistachio pudding mix
½ cup orange juice

½ cup water
4 eggs
½ cup vegetable oil
¾ cup chocolate syrup
Powdered sugar

Preheat oven to 350 degrees. In a large bowl, combine cake mix, pudding mix, orange juice, water, eggs, and oil. Blend to moisten. With an electric mixer on medium speed, beat for 2 minutes. Pour ¾ of the batter into a greased and floured tube pan. Add chocolate syrup to the remaining batter; mix well. Pour over batter in pan; don't stir. Bake for 1 hour. Allow to cool for 10 minutes. Remove from pan and dust with powdered sugar.

Chocolate Cake Balls

1 (18.25 ounce) package chocolate cake mix
1 (16 ounce) can chocolate frosting
1 (3 ounce) bar chocolate-flavored confectioners' coating

Prepare the cake mix according to package directions using any of the recommended pan sizes. When cake is done, crumble while warm into a large bowl; stir in the chocolate frosting until well blended. Place chocolate coating in a microwave-safe bowl. Microwave on HIGH for 1 minute; stir. Continue heating at 10 to 15 second intervals until melted and smooth. Use a melon baller or small scoop to form balls from the chocolate cake mixture. Dip the balls in chocolate using a toothpick. Place on waxed paper to set.

Chocolate Fudge Upside-Down Cake

2 tablespoons shortening
1 cup milk
1 teaspoon salt
2 teaspoons baking powder

1½ cups sugar
2 cups flour
1 teaspoon vanilla extract
3 tablespoons cocoa

TOPPING:
2 cups sugar
½ cup cocoa

2½ cups boiling water

Preheat oven to 375 degrees. Mix together all cake batter ingredients and place in cake pan; sprinkle with nuts if desired. Set aside. Topping: Mix sugar with cocoa and spread over batter in the pan. Then pour boiling water over top. Bake for 30 minutes.

Christmas Tree Cupcakes

1¾ cups flour
1 (4-serving size) package instant
   pistachio pudding mix
¾ cup mini chocolate chips
⅔ cup sugar
2½ teaspoons baking powder
½ teaspoon salt
2 eggs, beaten
1¼ cups milk

½ cup cooking oil
1 teaspoon vanilla extract
1 (16 ounce) can cream cheese
   frosting
Green and red colored sugar
   sprinkles
½ cup red and green candy-coated
   milk chocolate pieces

Preheat oven to 375 degrees. Line muffin cups with paper liners. In a large mixing bowl, stir together flour, pudding mix, chocolate chips, sugar, baking powder, and salt. In a small bowl, combine beaten eggs, milk, oil, and vanilla. Stir into the flour mixture until combined. Fill muffin cups ⅔ full. Bake for 18 to 20 minutes or until golden brown. Cool completely on a wire rack. Frost with cream cheese frosting. Sprinkle with red and green sugar then top with candy-coated milk chocolate pieces.

Chocolate Zucchini Cupcakes

2 (1 ounce) squares unsweetened
    chocolate, melted
3 eggs
1¾ cups brown sugar, packed
1 cup vegetable oil
2 cups flour
1 teaspoon baking powder

1 teaspoon baking soda
½ teaspoon salt
2 cups zucchini, grated
¾ cup walnuts, chopped
1 (16 ounce) can chocolate frosting
½ cup walnuts, halved

Preheat oven to 350 degrees. Line 24 muffin cups with paper liners; set aside. Melt chocolate and set aside. In a large bowl, beat eggs with sugar for about 10 minutes or until thickened. Blend oil and melted chocolate into the beaten egg mixture. In a small bowl, stir together flour, baking powder, baking soda, and salt; stir flour mixture into egg mixture until just blended. Stir in zucchini and chopped nuts. Using an ice cream scoop, spoon batter into prepared muffin cups. Bake for 20 minutes or until toothpick inserted in center comes out clean. Allow to cool completely before frosting. Garnish with walnut halves.

Black Bottom Cupcakes

1 (8 ounce) package cream cheese,
    softened
1 egg
1⅓ cup sugar, divided
⅛ and ½ teaspoon salt, divided
1 cup mini semisweet chocolate chips
1½ cups flour

¼ cup unsweetened cocoa powder
1 teaspoon baking soda
1 cup water
⅓ cup vegetable oil
1 tablespoon cider vinegar
1 teaspoon vanilla extract
1 (16 ounce) can chocolate frosting

Preheat oven to 350 degrees. Line muffin pans with paper liners. In a medium bowl, beat the cream cheese, egg, ⅓ cup sugar, and ⅛ teaspoon salt until light and fluffy. Stir in the chocolate chips and set aside. In a large bowl, mix together the flour, 1 cup sugar, cocoa, baking soda, and ½ teaspoon salt. Make a well in the center and add the water, oil, vinegar, and vanilla. Stir together until well blended. Fill muffin pans ⅓ full with the batter and top with a dollop of the cream cheese mixture. Bake for 25 to 30 minutes. Allow to cool completely before frosting.

Filled Chocolate Cupcakes

1 (18.5 ounce) package chocolate
    cake mix
1 (8 ounce) package cream cheese,
    softened
½ cup sugar

1 egg
1 cup semisweet chocolate chips
1 (16 ounce) can cream cheese
    frosting

Preheat oven to 350 degrees. Line muffin pans with paper liners; set aside. Prepare chocolate cake mix according to directions, but do not bake. In a separate bowl, cream together the cream cheese and sugar until smooth. Beat in the egg; stir until well blended. Stir in the chocolate chips. Fill muffin cups ⅓ full with chocolate cake batter. Add 1 teaspoon cream cheese mixture to center; top with more cake batter until ⅔ full. Repeat until batter is finished. Bake cupcakes according to package directions. Allow to cool completely before frosting.

Chocolate Brownie Cake

1 (18.25 ounce) package devil's food
   cake mix
1 (3.9 ounce) package instant
   chocolate pudding mix
4 eggs

1 cup sour cream
½ cup vegetable oil
½ cup water
2 cups semisweet chocolate chips
1 (16 ounce) can chocolate frosting

Preheat oven to 350 degrees. Grease and flour a 10 inch bundt pan. In a large bowl, stir together cake mix and pudding mix. Make a well in the center and pour in eggs, sour cream, oil, and water. Beat with an electric mixer on low speed until well blended. Scrape bowl, and beat 4 minutes on medium speed. Stir in chocolate chips. Pour batter into prepared pan. Bake for 50 to 60 minutes or until a toothpick inserted into the center comes out clean. Allow to cool completely before frosting.

Chocolate Caramel Cake

1⅔ cups flour
1½ cups sugar
⅔ cup cocoa
1½ teaspoons baking powder
1 teaspoon salt
1½ cups buttermilk

½ cup shortening
2 eggs
1½ teaspoons vanilla extract
30 caramels
1 can sweetened condensed milk

Preheat oven to 350 degrees. Beat first nine ingredients in large mixing bowl on low speed, scraping sides of bowl, until blended. Beat on high, scraping sides occasionally for an additional 3 minutes. Pour half of cake mix into a greased and floured 9x13 inch pan, and bake for 15 minutes. In the meantime, melt the caramels and sweetened condensed milk together. Spread over warm cake. Put remaining cake mixture on top of caramel mixture. Bake an additional 15 minutes or until done. May be served warm with vanilla ice cream for a real tasty treat.

Chocolate Applesauce Cake

1 (16 ounce) jar applesauce
1 (14 ounce) can sweetened
   condensed milk
½ cup butter, melted
3 eggs
1 (1 ounce) square unsweetened
   chocolate, melted

2 tablespoons vanilla extract
2½ cups buttermilk baking mix
½ teaspoon ground cinnamon
¾ cup walnuts, chopped
1 (16 ounce) can chocolate frosting

Preheat oven to 325 degrees. Grease a 10x15 inch baking pan. In a large mixing bowl, combine applesauce, sweetened condensed milk, butter, eggs, melted chocolate, and vanilla extract. Add the baking mix and cinnamon; blend well. Stir in the nuts. Pour batter into prepared pan. Bake for 25 to 30 minutes or until a toothpick inserted into the center comes out clean. Allow to cool completely before frosting.

Chocolate Cherry Shortcakes

2 cups buttermilk baking mix
⅓ cup baking cocoa
¼ cup and 2 tablespoons sugar
½ cup milk
¼ cup butter or margarine, melted

½ cup hot fudge topping
1 (21 ounce) can cherry pie filling, divided
1¼ cups frozen whipped topping, thawed

Preheat oven to 400 degrees. In a medium bowl, combine baking mix, cocoa, and sugar. Stir in milk and butter until soft dough forms. Drop dough into 4 equal mounds on an ungreased baking sheet. Bake for 15 minutes or until firm to the touch. Cool completely on wire rack. To assemble, cut shortcakes in half horizontally. Heat fudge topping until warm. Fill and top shortcakes with layers of fruit filling, whipped topping, and fudge topping. Serve immediately.

Earthquake Cake

1 cup nuts, chopped
1 cup coconut, finely chopped
1 package German chocolate
    cake mix

1 (8 ounce) package cream cheese
1 stick (¼ pound) shortening
1 pound powdered sugar

Preheat oven to 350 degrees. Grease 9x13 inch cake pan and put nuts and coconut in pan. Mix cake according to directions on package and add on top of nuts and coconut. Then beat together cream cheese, shortening, and powdered sugar until fluffy. Drop by spoonfuls all around on top of cake mix in pan. Bake for 40 minutes or until done when toothpick inserted in center comes out clean.

Chocolate Chip Cheesecake

1 (18 ounce) tube refrigerated
chocolate chip cookie dough,
cut into slices
3 (3 ounce) packages cream cheese,
softened

3 eggs
1 teaspoon vanilla extract
Nonstick cooking spray

Preheat oven to 350 degrees. Layer one-half of cookie dough slices on the bottom of a greased 9x13 inch baking dish. Bake according to package directions. While baking, beat cream cheese, eggs, and vanilla in a large mixing bowl until smooth. Spread over baked cookie dough. Top with remaining cookie dough slices. Bake for 35 more minutes.

Chocolate Chip Cookie Pie

2 eggs
½ cup flour
½ cup sugar
½ cup brown sugar, packed

1 cup butter, melted
1 cup semisweet chocolate chips
1 cup pecans, chopped
1 (9 inch) pie shell

Preheat oven to 325 degrees. In a large bowl, beat eggs until light and foamy. Add the flour, sugar, and brown sugar; beat until well blended. Blend in melted butter. Stir in the chocolate chips and nuts. Pour mixture into prepared pie shell. Bake for 1 hour. Serve warm with whipped topping or ice cream.

Cherry Chocolate Pie

1 (9 inch) piecrust, baked
2 (21 ounce) cans cherry pie filling
½ cup sliced almonds
1 tablespoon butter

3 tablespoons semisweet baker's
chocolate
Whipped topping
Chocolate syrup

Preheat oven to 350 degrees. Spoon pie filling into cooled piecrust. Bake for
30 to 35 minutes or until bubbly. Allow to cool. Sprinkle almonds over top and
set aside. In a double boiler, melt butter and chocolate, stirring constantly. Pour
chocolate mixture over pie. Garnish with whipped cream and chocolate syrup.

German Chocolate Pie

1 cup sugar, divided
3 tablespoons cornstarch
1½ cups milk
1 (4 ounce) bar German sweet
  chocolate, chopped
1 tablespoon and ¼ cup butter,
  divided

2 egg yolks, beaten
1 teaspoon vanilla extract
1 (9 inch) piecrust, baked
1 egg
1 (5 ounce) can evaporated milk
1⅓ cups flaked coconut
½ cup pecans, chopped

In a medium saucepan, combine the ½ cup sugar and the cornstarch. Stir in the milk, chocolate, and 1 tablespoon butter. Cook and stir until thick and bubbly. Reduce heat; cook and stir 2 minutes more. Gradually stir in egg yolks. Bring to boiling. Cook and stir 2 minutes more; stir in vanilla. Turn the hot pie filling into the baked pie shell. In another saucepan, combine egg, evaporated milk, ½ cup sugar, and ¼ cup butter. Cook and stir over medium heat until the mixture is thick and bubbly. Stir in the coconut and pecans. Spread the pecan mixture evenly over the chocolate filling. Cool the pie on a wire rack. Chill thoroughly in the refrigerator.

Chocolate Banana Pie

1 (8 ounce) package cream cheese,
  softened
1 cup powdered sugar
1 (9 inch) baked pie shell
1 (13.9 ounce) package instant
  chocolate pudding mix

1 cup heavy whipping cream
½ cup sugar
2 large bananas, sliced
½ cup pecans, chopped

In a large bowl, beat the cream cheese and powdered sugar until smooth. Press into the prepared pie shell. Prepare chocolate pudding according to package directions, but use ½ cup less milk; set aside. Whip the cream with ½ cup sugar. Spread half of the whipped cream over the cream cheese in the pie shell. Lay sliced bananas on top of the whipped cream and cover with the chocolate pudding. Spread the other half of the whipped cream over the pudding layer. Sprinkle with chopped pecans. Refrigerate at least 3 hours before serving.

Chocolate Dream Pie

1 (12 ounce) can evaporated milk
2 egg yolks
2 cups semisweet chocolate chips

1 (9 inch) graham cracker piecrust
Whipped topping

In a medium saucepan over medium-low heat, whisk together evaporated milk and egg yolks; stirring constantly. Cook until mixture is very hot and thickens slightly but does not boil. Remove from heat and stir in chocolate chips until completely melted and mixture is smooth. Pour into crust. Refrigerate for 3 hours or until firm. Garnish with whipped topping before serving.

French Silk Chocolate Pie

1 cup butter
1½ cups sugar
4 tablespoons unsweetened
  cocoa powder

2 teaspoons vanilla extract
4 eggs
1 (9 inch) baked piecrust

In a large bowl, cream together the butter and sugar. Blend in the cocoa and vanilla. With an electric mixer on high speed, beat in one egg until thoroughly blended. Repeat with each remaining egg. Keep whipping until fluffy. Spread mixture into the prepared pie shell. Refrigerate until chilled.

Heavenly Chocolate Pie

⅔ cup sugar
⅓ cup cornstarch
½ teaspoon salt
4 egg yolks
3 cups milk
1 tablespoon vanilla extract

2 tablespoons butter or margarine,
   softened
2 cups dark chocolate chips, divided
1 (9 inch) baked pie shell
1 (12 ounce) container frozen
   whipped topping, thawed

In a 2 quart saucepan, stir together sugar, cornstarch, and salt. Combine egg yolks and milk in a container with a pouring spout. Gradually blend milk mixture into sugar mixture. Cook over medium heat, stirring constantly, until mixture comes to a boil. Boil and stir for 1 minute. Remove from heat; stir in the vanilla and butter. Add 1¾ cups chocolate chips; stir until chips are melted and mixture is well blended. Pour into prepared pie shell. Refrigerate until chilled and firm. Garnish with whipped topping and remaining chocolate chips.

Chocolate Banana Cream Pie

2 (1 ounce) squares semisweet
   chocolate
1 tablespoon milk
1 tablespoon butter
1 (9 inch) deep dish piecrust,
   baked and cooled
2 bananas, sliced

1½ cups cold milk
1 (3.5 ounce) package instant
   vanilla pudding mix
1½ cups shredded coconut
1½ cups frozen whipped topping,
   thawed
2 tablespoons flaked coconut,
   toasted

Combine chocolate, 1 tablespoon milk, and butter or margarine in a medium, microwave-safe bowl. Microwave on HIGH for 1 to 1½ minutes, stirring every 30 seconds. Stir until chocolate is completely melted. Spread evenly in piecrust. Arrange banana slices over chocolate. Pour 1½ cups milk into a large bowl. Add pudding mix, and beat with wire whisk for 2 minutes. Stir in 1½ cups coconut. Spoon over banana slices in crust. Spread whipped topping over pie. Sprinkle with toasted coconut. Refrigerate 4 hours, or until set. Store in refrigerator.

Double Layer
Chocolate Peanut Butter Pie

½ (8 ounce) package cream cheese,
   softened
1 tablespoon sugar
1 tablespoon cold milk
1 cup peanut butter
1 (8 ounce) container frozen
   whipped topping, thawed

1 (9 inch) prepared graham cracker
   crust
2 (3.9 ounce) packages instant
   chocolate pudding mix
2 cups cold milk
4 peanut butter cups, cut into
   ½ inch pieces

In a large bowl, combine cream cheese, sugar, 1 tablespoon milk, and peanut butter until smooth. Gently stir in 1½ cups of whipped topping. Spread mixture on the bottom of the piecrust. In a medium bowl, stir pudding mix with 2 cups milk until thick. Immediately stir in remaining whipped topping. Spread mixture over peanut butter layer. Scatter peanut butter cups over top of pie. Cover and refrigerate overnight.

Chocolate Malted Pie

2 (3.5 ounce) packages non-instant
   chocolate pudding mix
3 cups milk
4 (1 ounce) squares bittersweet
   chocolate
⅓ cup malted milk powder

1 (9 inch) prepared graham
   cracker crust
1 cup heavy whipping cream
1 teaspoon sugar
¾ cup chocolate covered malted
   milk balls, cut into pieces
2 tablespoons chocolate syrup

Cook pudding according to package directions, using the 3 cups of milk. Remove from heat. Add the bittersweet chocolate and stir in the malted milk powder. Cool mixture for 5 minutes, stirring often. Pour mixture into the prepared crust. Cover and refrigerate for 2 hours.

One hour before serving: Beat the cream and sugar with an electric mixer until soft peaks form when beaters are lifted. Spread the whipped cream over the chocolate filling. Sprinkle the chopped malted milk balls over the top of the pie. Drizzle the chocolate syrup over the pie. Refrigerate until ready to serve.

Chocolate Chip Walnut Pie

¾ cup light brown sugar, packed
½ cup flour
½ teaspoon baking powder
¼ teaspoon ground cinnamon
2 eggs, lightly beaten
1 cup semisweet chocolate chips
1 cup walnuts, coarsely chopped

1 (9 inch) baked pie shell
½ cup heavy cream, chilled
1 tablespoon powdered sugar
¼ teaspoon vanilla extract
¼ teaspoon ground cinnamon
1 pinch ground nutmeg

Preheat oven to 350 degrees. In a large bowl, stir together brown sugar, flour, baking powder, and ¼ teaspoon cinnamon. Add the eggs and stir until well blended. Stir in the chocolate chips and walnuts. Pour mixture into prepared pie shell. Bake for 25 to 30 minutes or until lightly browned and set. Serve slightly warm with spiced cream.

SPICED CREAM: In a medium bowl, mix together cream, powdered sugar, vanilla, ¼ teaspoon cinnamon, and nutmeg. Whip until light and fluffy.

Double Chocolate Layer Cheesecake

2 (8 ounce) packages cream cheese,
    softened
½ cup sugar
½ teaspoon vanilla extract

2 eggs
3 squares semisweet chocolate,
    melted, slightly cooled
1 (9 inch) chocolate piecrust

Preheat oven to 350 degrees. In a large bowl, mix cream cheese, sugar, and vanilla with an electric mixer on medium speed. Mix until well blended. Add the eggs; beat until well blended. Stir melted chocolate into 1 cup of the batter. Pour chocolate batter into the piecrust. Top with the plain batter. Bake for 40 minutes or until center is almost set. Allow to cool. Refrigerate overnight before serving.

Chocolate Raspberry Cheese Pie

2 (3 ounce) packages cream cheese, softened
1 (14 ounce) can sweetened condensed milk
1 egg
3 tablespoons lemon juice
1 teaspoon vanilla extract
1 cup fresh or frozen raspberries
1 (9 inch) chocolate piecrust
2 (1 ounce) bars semisweet baking chocolate
¼ cup whipping cream

Preheat oven to 350 degrees. In a large bowl, beat cream cheese until fluffy. Gradually beat in condensed milk until smooth. Add egg, lemon juice and vanilla; mix well. Arrange raspberries on bottom of crust. Slowly pour cheese mixture over fruit. Bake for 30 to 35 minutes or until center is almost set. Cool. In a small saucepan over low heat, melt chocolate with whipping cream. Cook and stir until thickened and smooth. Remove from heat. Top cheesecake with chocolate glaze. Allow to chill before serving.

Chocolate Bar Pie

4 ounces cream cheese, softened
1¾ cups and 1 tablespoon milk, divided
2 (12 ounce) containers frozen whipped topping, thawed and divided

2 (2.7 ounce) chocolate-covered caramel peanut nougat candy bars, chopped
1 (3.4 ounce) package instant chocolate pudding mix
1 (9 inch) chocolate piecrust

In a large bowl, mix cream cheese and 1 tablespoon milk with wire whisk until smooth. Gently stir in 2 cups whipped topping and chopped candy bars; set aside. In a medium bowl, add 1¾ cups milk and pudding mix. Beat with wire whisk for 1 minute. Gently stir in ½ cup whipped topping. Spread half of the pudding mixture on bottom of crust. Spread cream cheese mixture over pudding mixture. Top with remaining pudding mixture. Refrigerate for 4 hours or until pie is set. Garnish with remaining whipped topping.

Chocolate Triple Layer Pie

2 cups cold milk
2 (3.4 ounce) packages instant
chocolate pudding mix
1 (9 inch) graham cracker piecrust

1 (8 ounce) container frozen
whipped topping, thawed and
divided

In a large bowl, combine milk and pudding mixes. Beat with a wire whisk for 1 minute. Spoon 1½ cups of the pudding into crust. Gently stir half of the whipped topping into remaining pudding. Spread over pudding in crust. Top with remaining whipped topping. Refrigerate for 4 hours or until set.

Chocolate Peanut Butter Pie

2 (4 ounce) packages single serve
    ready-made chocolate pudding
⅓ cup peanut butter

1 (8 ounce) container frozen
    whipped topping, thawed
1 (9 inch) prepared graham
    cracker crust

In a large bowl, combine pudding and peanut butter; stir until smooth. Fold in whipped topping; stir until completely blended. Pour filling into piecrust. Freeze pie until firm. Partially thaw in refrigerator before serving.

Chocolate Pecan Pie

2 squares unsweetened chocolate
2 tablespoons butter
3 eggs
½ cup sugar

¾ cup dark corn syrup (may use
    same amount of light syrup)
1 cup pecans, halved
1 (9 inch) pie shell

Preheat oven to 350 degrees. Melt chocolate and butter together. Beat eggs, sugar, chocolate mixture, and corn syrup together. Mix in pecans. Pour into pastry-lined pie pan. Bake 40 to 50 minutes, just until set. Serve slightly warm, or cold, with ice cream or whipped topping.

Away in a manger, no crib for a bed,
The little Lord Jesus laid down his sweet head.
The stars in the sky looked down where he lay,
The little Lord Jesus asleep in the hay.

Good news from heaven the angels bring,
Glad tidings to the earth they sing:
To us this day a child is given,
To crown us with the joy of heaven.

MARTIN LUTHER

Holiday Candy and Fudge

And it came to pass, as the angels were gone away from them into heaven, the shepherds said one to another, let us now go even unto Bethlehem, and see this thing which is come to pass, which the Lord hath made known unto us. And they came with haste, and found Mary, Joseph, and the babe lying in a manger.

LUKE 2:15–16

Homemade Turtles

1 (18 ounce) package semisweet
  chocolate chips
1 (7 ounce) jar marshmallow cream
1 (14 ounce) can sweetened condensed
  milk

1 teaspoon vanilla extract
1 pound walnuts, chopped
40 caramels, unwrapped

In a medium saucepan, combine chocolate chips, marshmallow cream, and milk. Cook over low heat; stirring constantly until melted. Remove from heat; stir in the vanilla and walnuts. Slice each caramel into 6 equal pieces; fold in. Drop by teaspoonfuls onto waxed paper. Allow to cool completely.

Chinese New Year Chocolate Candy

2 cups semisweet chocolate chips

2 cups butterscotch chips

2½ cups dry-roasted peanuts

4 cups chow mein noodles

Grease a 9x13 inch baking dish. Melt chocolate and butterscotch chips in the top of a double boiler over simmering water. Remove from heat and stir in peanuts. Stir in noodles until everything is well coated. Press into prepared dish. Chill until set; cut into squares.

Chocolate Walnut Fudge

4½ cups sugar
1 (12 ounce) can evaporated milk
1 (12 ounce) package semisweet
  chocolate chips

1½ cups butter
1 teaspoon vanilla extract
½ cup walnuts, chopped

Grease an 8x8 inch pan; set aside. In a large saucepan, combine sugar and milk; boil for 6 minutes. Remove from heat. Add the chocolate chips, butter, and vanilla. Beat for 10 minutes with an electric mixer on medium speed. Add the nuts. Pour into prepared pan. Refrigerate until set.

Buckeyes

1½ cups peanut butter
½ cup butter, softened
1 teaspoon vanilla extract
4 cups powdered sugar, sifted
6 ounces semisweet chocolate chips
2 tablespoons shortening

Line a baking sheet with waxed paper; set aside. In a medium bowl, mix peanut butter, butter, vanilla, and powdered sugar with hands to form a smooth, stiff dough. Shape into balls using 2 teaspoons of dough for each ball. Place on prepared pan; refrigerate. Melt shortening and chocolate together in the top of a double boiler. Stir occasionally until smooth; remove from heat. Remove balls from refrigerator. Insert a wooden toothpick into a ball and dip into melted chocolate mixture. Return to wax paper, chocolate side down; remove toothpick. Repeat with remaining balls. Refrigerate for 30 minutes to set.

Cookie Bark

1 (20 ounce) package chocolate sandwich cookies with cream filling
2 (18.5 ounce) packages white chocolate

Line a 10x15 inch jelly roll pan with waxed paper. Coat paper with a nonstick cooking spray; set aside. Break half of the cookies into coarse pieces and place in a large bowl. In a microwave-safe bowl, melt one package of the white chocolate in the microwave. Quickly fold melted chocolate into the broken cookie pieces. Pour the mixture into the prepared pan and spread to cover half of the pan. Repeat the process with the remaining chocolate and cookies. Refrigerate until solid. Remove from the pan and carefully peel off the waxed paper. Place bark on a large cutting board and cut into pieces with a large knife. Store in an air-tight container.

Rocky Road Fudge

1 (12 ounce) package semisweet
   chocolate chips
1 (14 ounce) can sweetened
   condensed milk

1 teaspoon vanilla extract
3 cups miniature marshmallows
1½ cups walnuts, coarsely chopped

Line a 9x13 inch baking pan with foil; grease lightly. In a large, microwave-safe bowl, add chocolate chips and sweetened condensed milk. Microwave on HIGH power for 1 minute; stir. Microwave at additional 10 to 20 second intervals, stirring until smooth. Stir in vanilla extract. Fold in marshmallows and nuts. Press mixture into prepared baking pan. Refrigerate until ready to serve. Lift from pan and remove foil; cut into pieces.

Chocolate Pudding Fudge

1 (3.5 ounce) package non-instant
  chocolate pudding mix
⅓ cup sugar

½ cup brown sugar
½ cup heavy cream
1 tablespoon butter

Generously grease an 8x8 inch square baking pan. In a large, microwave-safe bowl, combine pudding mix, sugar, brown sugar, and cream. Microwave on HIGH power until it boils, about 4 minutes. Continue to boil in microwave about 3 minutes more. Stir in butter and beat until mixture begins to thicken. Spread into prepared pan and allow to cool completely before cutting into squares.

Cherry Chocolate Fudge

1 (14 ounce) can sweetened
   condensed milk
1 (12 ounce) package semisweet
   chocolate chips
½ cup almonds, chopped

½ cup candied cherries, chopped
1 teaspoon almond extract
¼ cup pecans, halved
¼ cup candied cherries, halved

Line an 8x8 inch square pan with aluminum foil. In a microwave-safe bowl, combine sweetened condensed milk and chocolate chips. Microwave on HIGH for 1½ minutes, or until chocolate is melted; stir until smooth. Stir in chopped almonds, chopped cherries, and almond extract. Pour into prepared pan and spread evenly. Place pecan halves and cherry halves on top. Cover and refrigerate for 2 hours or until firm. Cut into 1 inch squares.

Cinnamon Fudge

1 pound powdered sugar
½ cup unsweetened cocoa
¼ teaspoon ground cinnamon
½ cup butter

¼ cup milk
1½ teaspoons vanilla extract
1 cup nuts, chopped

Line an 8x8 inch baking pan with foil, allowing foil to extend over sides. Grease the foil. In a large bowl, mix together sugar, cocoa, and cinnamon; set aside. In a medium saucepan, heat butter and milk until butter melts. Remove from heat; add vanilla extract. Pour butter mixture into sugar mixture. Stir in the nuts. Pour into prepared pan. Refrigerate for at least 1 hour. Use foil to lift fudge out of pan. Cut into 2 inch squares.

White Chocolate Candy Cane Fudge

2 (10 ounce) packages white
    chocolate chips
1 (14 ounce) can sweetened
    condensed milk

½ teaspoon peppermint extract
1 dash red food coloring
1½ cups candy canes, crushed

Line an 8x8 inch baking pan with aluminum foil. Grease the foil. Combine the white chocolate chips and sweetened condensed milk in a saucepan over medium heat. Stir frequently until almost melted, remove from heat and continue to stir until smooth. When chips are completely melted, stir in the peppermint extract, food coloring, and candy canes. Spread evenly in the bottom of the prepared pan. Chill for 2 hours before cutting into squares.

Chocolate Almond Fudge

4 cups sugar
1 (7 ounce) jar marshmallow crème
1 (12 ounce) can evaporated milk
1 tablespoon butter
2 cups semisweet chocolate chips

1 (7 ounce) milk chocolate bar,
   broken into pieces
1 teaspoon vanilla extract
¾ cup toasted almonds, chopped

Line an 8x8 inch square baking pan with foil, extending foil over edges of pan. In a heavy 4-quart saucepan, stir together sugar, marshmallow crème, evaporated milk, and butter. Cook over medium heat, stirring constantly, until mixture comes to full rolling boil. Allow to boil for 7 minutes, stirring constantly. Remove from heat; immediately add chocolate chips and chocolate bar pieces, stirring until chocolate is melted and mixture is smooth. Stir in vanilla and almonds. Pour mixture into prepared pan; cool until firm. Use foil to lift fudge from pan. Cut into 1 inch squares.

Peppermint Chocolate Fudge

2 cups milk chocolate chips
1 cup semisweet chocolate chips
1 (14 ounce) can sweetened
   condensed milk

Dash of salt
½ teaspoon peppermint extract
¾ cup hard peppermint
   candy, crushed

Line an 8x8 inch square pan with foil. Grease foil. In a saucepan, over low heat, melt milk chocolate chips, semisweet chocolate chips, sweetened condensed milk, and salt. Remove from heat; stir in peppermint extract. Spread evenly into prepared pan. Sprinkle with peppermint candy. Chill for 2 hours or until firm. Turn fudge onto cutting board and cut into squares.

Cranberry Chocolate Fudge

1 (12 ounce) package fresh or
   frozen cranberries
½ cup light corn syrup
2 cups semisweet chocolate chips

½ cup powdered sugar
¼ cup evaporated milk
1 teaspoon vanilla extract

Line bottom and sides of an 8x8 inch pan with plastic wrap; set aside. In a medium saucepan, bring cranberries and corn syrup to a boil. Boil on high for 5 to 7 minutes, stirring occasionally, until the liquid is reduced to about 3 tablespoons. Remove from heat. Immediately add chocolate chips, stirring until they are melted completely. Add powdered sugar, evaporated milk, and vanilla extract; stir until mixture is thick and glossy. Pour into pan. Cover and chill until firm.

Chocolate Butterscotch Fudge

1½ cups sugar
⅔ cup evaporated milk
2 tablespoons butter
¼ teaspoon salt
1 (7 ounce) jar marshmallow crème

¾ cup semisweet chocolate chips
¾ cup butterscotch chips
½ cup pecans, chopped
1 teaspoon vanilla extract

Line an 8x8 inch square baking pan with foil. In a heavy saucepan over medium heat, combine sugar, evaporated milk, butter, and salt. Bring to a boil and let roll 5 minutes. Remove from heat and stir in marshmallow crème, chocolate chips, butterscotch chips, pecans, and vanilla. Continue stirring until marshmallow crème is melted and all ingredients are thoroughly combined. Pour into prepared dish. Refrigerate for 2 hours, until firm. Lift from dish, remove foil, and cut into pieces.

Heavenly Christmas Fudge

1 cup sugar
¼ cup baking cocoa
¼ cup butter
⅓ cup milk

1 tablespoon corn syrup
⅓ cup nuts, chopped
1 teaspoon vanilla extract
2¼ cups powdered sugar

Grease a 9x5 inch loaf pan; set aside. In a 2 quart saucepan, combine the sugar and cocoa. Stir in the butter, milk, and corn syrup. Heat to boiling over medium heat; stirring frequently. Boil and stir one minute; remove from heat. Allow to cool without stirring until bottom of pan is just warm; about 45 minutes. Stir in nuts and vanilla. Blend in the powdered sugar until mixture is very stiff; press into prepared loaf pan. Refrigerate until firm. Cut fudge into festive shapes with cookie cutters.

Quick Chocolate Truffles

2 (10 to 12 ounce) packages milk chocolate chips
1 (8 ounce) carton frozen whipped topping, thawed
1¼ cups graham cracker crumbs

Microwave chocolate chips on medium-high heat for 1 minute. Stir; microwave 10 to 20 seconds longer until chips are melted. Stir occasionally during melting process. Allow to cool for about 30 minutes; stir occasionally. Fold in whipped topping. Drop rounded teaspoonfuls onto waxed paper–lined cookie sheets. Freeze until firm, about 1½ hours. Shape into balls and roll in crushed graham crackers. Refrigerate in airtight containers. If desired, you may freeze truffles and remove from freezer 30 minutes before serving.

Joy to the world, the Lord is come!
Let earth receive her King;
Let every heart prepare Him room,
And Heaven and nature sing,
And Heaven and nature sing,
And Heaven, and Heaven, and nature sing.

Party Mixes and Snacks

And so it was, that, while they were there, the days were accomplished that she should be delivered. And she brought forth her firstborn son, and wrapped him in swaddling clothes, and laid him in a manger; because there was no room for them in the inn.

Luke 2:6–7

White Chocolate Party Mix

1 (10 ounce) package mini pretzels
5 cups doughnut-shaped oat cereal
5 cups bite-sized crispy corn cereal
   squares
1¾ cups salted peanuts

1 pound candy-coated chocolate
   pieces
2 (12 ounce) packages white
   chocolate chips
3 tablespoons vegetable oil

Preheat oven to 170 degrees. In a large bowl, add pretzels, cereals, peanuts, and chocolate pieces; toss until well combined. Set aside. Put white chocolate chips and oil in a baking pan and bake until melted; stirring often. Pour over cereal mixture. Stir until well coated. Spread onto waxed paper. Allow to cool completely before breaking into pieces.

Muddy Buddy Party Mix

½ cup butter
½ cup peanut butter
1 cup milk chocolate chips
1 teaspoon vanilla extract

1 (12 ounce) package rice
squares cereal
1 pound powdered sugar

In a saucepan, over medium heat, melt butter, peanut butter, chocolate chips, and vanilla. Pour cereal in a large bowl. Pour melted chocolate mixture over cereal. Stir gently until cereal is evenly coated. Slowly pour powdered sugar over mix and stir until evenly coated. Spread on waxed paper to cool. Store in an airtight container.

Chocolate Party Mix

2 cups corn cereal squares
2 cups small pretzel twists
1 cup dry-roasted peanuts

20 caramels, unwrapped and
  coarsely chopped
1 (11.5 ounce) package milk
  chocolate chips

Coat a 9x13 inch baking pan with nonstick cooking spray. In a large bowl, combine cereal, pretzels, peanuts, and caramels. Microwave chocolate chips in a microwave-safe bowl on HIGH power for 1 minute; stir. Microwave at additional 10 to 20 second intervals, stirring until smooth. Pour over cereal mixture; stir to coat evenly. Spread mixture into prepared baking pan; cool for 30 to 45 minutes or until firm. Break into bite-sized pieces.

Christmas Snack Mix

1 (16 ounce) jar dry-roasted peanuts
2 (14 ounce) packages red and green candy-coated chocolate pieces
1 (14 ounce) package red and green candy-coated chocolate covered peanuts
1 (7 ounce) jar wheat nuts

Mix together the peanuts, candy-coated chocolate pieces, candy-coated chocolate peanuts, and wheat nuts. Serve in a large bowl or place in decorative glass jars to give as gifts.

White Chocolate Covered Pretzels

6 (1 ounce) squares white chocolate
1 (15 ounce) package mini twist pretzels
¼ cup red and green candy sprinkles

Melt white chocolate in the top of a double boiler, stirring constantly. Dip pretzel into the white chocolate, completely covering half of the pretzel. Roll in candy sprinkles and lay on waxed paper to dry. Continue process until all of the chocolate is gone. Place pretzels in refrigerator for 15 minutes to harden.

Milk Chocolate Popcorn

12 cups popcorn, popped
2½ cups salted peanuts
¼ cup butter

1 (11.5 ounce) package milk
    chocolate chips
1 cup light corn syrup

Preheat oven to 300 degrees. Grease a large roasting pan. Line a large serving plate with waxed paper. Combine popcorn and nuts in prepared roasting pan. In a medium saucepan, combine butter, chocolate chips, and corn syrup. Cook over medium heat, stirring constantly, until mixture boils. Pour chocolate mixture over popcorn; toss well to coat. Bake, stirring frequently, for 30 to 40 minutes. Cool slightly in pan before removing to prepared serving plate.

Grilled S'Mores

4 graham cracker squares, divided
   in half crosswise
4 marshmallows

2 milk chocolate candy bars,
   divided in half crosswise

Top one graham cracker square with one candy bar half, one marshmallow, and another graham cracker square half. Repeat with remaining ingredients. Center each S'More on an 8x12 inch aluminum foil sheet. Wrap and seal, leaving room for heat to circulate inside the packets. Grill covered for 4 to 5 minutes or until the marshmallows are melted.

Chocolate Cake and Fruit Kabobs

2 cups semisweet chocolate chips
2 tablespoons shortening
24 bite-sized pieces pound cake
24 bite-sized pieces fresh fruit
   (pineapple, banana, strawberries)

1 (10 ounce) package frozen
   strawberries in syrup, thawed
4 tablespoons sugar

In a medium, microwave-safe bowl, microwave the chocolate chips and shortening on HIGH for 1 minute; stir. Microwave at additional 10 to 20 second intervals, stirring until smooth. Dip cake pieces into chocolate mixture; shake off excess. Place on a waxed paper–lined baking sheet. Drizzle the tops of chocolate dipped cakes with the additional chocolate. Refrigerate until set. On skewers, alternate the chocolate coated cakes with pieces of fruit; refrigerate. In a blender, puree strawberries and sugar until smooth. Serve with kabobs.

Chocolate Chip Cookie Brittle

1 cup butter
1 cup sugar
1½ teaspoons vanilla extract
1 teaspoon salt

2 cups flour
2 cups semisweet chocolate chips
1 cup nuts, chopped

Preheat oven to 375 degrees. In a large bowl, beat butter, sugar, vanilla extract, and salt. Gradually beat in flour. Stir in 1½ cups chocolate chips and nuts. Press mixture into an ungreased 10x15 inch jelly roll pan. Bake for 20 to 25 minutes or until golden brown and set. Cool until just slightly warm. Microwave the remaining chocolate chips in a small, heavy-duty plastic bag on HIGH for 30 to 45 seconds; knead. Microwave at additional 10 to 20 second intervals, kneading until smooth. Cut tiny corner from bag; squeeze to drizzle over cookie. Allow chocolate to cool and set; break cookies into pieces.

Chocolate Pizza

1 (12 ounce) package semisweet
   chocolate chips
1 pound white almond bark, divided
2 cups miniature marshmallows
1 cup crisp rice cereal
1 cup peanuts

1 (6 ounce) jar red maraschino
   cherries, drained and cut in half
3 tablespoons green maraschino
   cherries, drained and quartered
½ cup coconut
1 teaspoon vegetable oil

In a large saucepan over low heat, melt chocolate chips with 14 ounces of almond bark, stirring until smooth; remove from heat. Stir in the marshmallows, cereal, and peanuts. Pour onto a greased 12 inch pizza pan. Top with cherries and sprinkle with coconut. Melt remaining 2 ounces of bark with oil over low heat, stirring until smooth. Drizzle mixture over coconut. Chill until firm.

Mint Chocolate Chip Cheese Ball

1 (12 ounce) package mini semisweet chocolate chips
1 (12 ounce) package peppermint candies, crushed
1 (8 ounce) package cream cheese, softened
8 ounces pecans, chopped

In a large bowl, blend chocolate chips, peppermint candies, and cream cheese. Form mixture into a large ball. Roll ball in pecans until evenly coated. Serve with chocolate sugar wafers.

Good news from heaven the angels bring, Glad tidings to the earth they sing:
To us this day a child is given, To crown us with the joy of heaven.

MARTIN LUTHER

Christmas Morning
Breakfast Foods

And she shall bring forth a son,
and thou shalt call his name JESUS:
for he shall save his people from their sins.

MATTHEW 1:21

Chocolate Chip Pancakes

2 cups buttermilk biscuit baking mix
1 egg
1 cup milk
1 tablespoon sugar

½ cup mini chocolate chips
Whipped topping
Maple syrup

In a large bowl, mix biscuit mix, egg, milk, and sugar until smooth. Fold in the chocolate chips. Heat greased skillet over medium heat. Spoon batter onto skillet and cook until bubbles begin to appear and edges appear dry. Flip and cook until golden brown. Use whipped topping to garnish. Serve with warm maple syrup.

Gingerbread Waffles
with Hot Chocolate Sauce

1 cup light molasses
½ cup butter
1½ teaspoons baking soda
1½ cups milk
1 egg

2 cups flour
1½ teaspoons ground ginger
½ teaspoon ground cinnamon
½ teaspoon salt

HOT CHOCOLATE SAUCE:

2 cups boiling water
1 cup sugar
2 tablespoons cornstarch
½ cup unsweetened cocoa powder

1 teaspoon salt
2 teaspoons vanilla extract
2 tablespoons butter
Whipped topping

Preheat waffle iron and spray with nonstick cooking spray. In a small saucepan, heat molasses and ½ cup butter until almost boiling. Remove from heat and let cool slightly. Stir in the baking soda, milk, and egg. In a large bowl, mix flour, ginger, cinnamon, and salt. Make a well in the center and pour in the molasses mixture. Mix until smooth. Pour the mix onto hot waffle iron. Cook until golden brown. Serve with hot chocolate sauce.

Hot chocolate sauce: In a medium saucepan, combine boiling water, 1 cup sugar, cornstarch, cocoa powder, and 1 teaspoon salt. Cook over medium heat, stirring constantly, until mixture comes to a boil. Remove from heat and add vanilla and 2 tablespoons butter; stir until smooth. Pour chocolate sauce over hot waffles and garnish with whipped topping.

Chocolate Waffles

2¼ cups flour
½ cup sugar
1 tablespoon baking powder
¾ teaspoon salt
1 cup semisweet chocolate chips
¾ cup butter

1½ cups milk
3 eggs
1 tablespoon vanilla extract
Whipped topping
Chocolate shavings
Maple syrup

Preheat waffle iron. In a large bowl, combine flour, sugar, baking powder, and salt. In a medium, microwave-safe bowl, microwave chocolate chips and butter on HIGH for 1 minute; stir. Microwave at additional 10 to 20 second intervals, stirring until smooth. Cool to room temperature. Stir in milk, eggs, and vanilla extract. Add chocolate mixture to flour mixture; stir. Cook batter in waffle iron. Serve warm. Garnish with whipped topping and chocolate shavings. Serve with warm maple syrup.

Chocolate Chip Banana Muffins

1 cup margarine
1¼ cups sugar
1 egg
3 ripe bananas
1 tablespoon instant coffee granules,
    dissolved in 1 tablespoon water

1 teaspoon vanilla extract
2¼ cups flour
¼ teaspoon salt
1 teaspoon baking powder
1 teaspoon baking soda
1 cup semisweet chocolate chips

Preheat oven to 350 degrees. Blend together margarine, sugar, egg, banana, coffee, and vanilla in blender or food processor for 2 minutes. Add flour, salt, baking powder, and baking soda. Blend just until flour disappears. Add chocolate chips and mix in with a wooden spoon. Spoon mixture into 18 paper-lined muffin cups. Bake for 25 minutes.

Chocolate Chip Pumpkin Muffins

¾ cup sugar
¼ cup vegetable oil
2 eggs
¾ cup canned pumpkin puree
¼ cup water
1½ cups flour
¾ teaspoon baking powder

½ teaspoon baking soda
¼ teaspoon ground cloves
½ teaspoon ground cinnamon
¼ teaspoon salt
¼ teaspoon ground nutmeg
½ cup semisweet chocolate chips

Preheat oven to 400 degrees. Line muffin pans with paper liners. In a large bowl, mix sugar, vegetable oil, and eggs. Add pumpkin and water. In a medium bowl, combine the flour, baking powder, baking soda, cloves, cinnamon, salt, and nutmeg. Pour flour mixture into pumpkin mixture and stir until well blended. Stir in the chocolate chips. Fill muffin cups ⅔ full with batter. Bake for 20 to 25 minutes.

Chocolate Chip Muffins

2 cups flour
½ cup and 3 tablespoons sugar, divided
3 teaspoons baking powder
¾ cup mini semisweet chocolate chips

½ teaspoon salt
¾ cup milk
⅓ cup vegetable oil
1 egg
2 tablespoons brown sugar

Preheat oven to 400 degrees. Line muffin pan with baking cups. In a medium bowl, combine flour, ½ cup sugar, baking powder, chocolate chips, and salt; mix well. In a small bowl, combine milk, oil, and egg; blend well. Pour milk mixture into flour mixture and stir until dry ingredients are moistened. Fill muffin cups ⅔ full. Sprinkle tops of muffins with combination of 3 tablespoons sugar and 2 tablespoons brown sugar. Bake for 20 to 25 minutes or until toothpick inserted in center comes out clean. Allow to cool for 3 minutes before removing from pan.

Raspberry White Chocolate Muffins

1 cup milk
½ and ¼ cup butter, melted and divided
1 egg, slightly beaten
2 cups flour
⅓ and ¼ cup sugar, divided

1 tablespoon baking powder
1 teaspoon salt
1 cup fresh or frozen raspberries
½ cup white chocolate chips

Preheat oven to 400 degrees. Line a muffin pan with paper liners. In a large bowl, combine milk, butter, and egg. Stir in flour, ⅓ cup sugar, baking powder, and salt; stir just until flour is moistened. Gently stir in raspberries and white chocolate chips. Spoon batter into prepared baking cups. Bake for 24 to 28 minutes or until golden brown. Allow to cool slightly before removing from pan. Dip top of each muffin in melted butter, then in sugar.

Double Chocolate Chip Nut Muffins

2 cups flour
½ cup unsweetened cocoa
    powder
1½ cups and 4 tablespoons sugar,
    divided
½ teaspoon baking soda
2 teaspoons baking powder
¼ teaspoon salt

1¼ cups milk
1 egg
2 tablespoons vegetable oil
1 teaspoon vanilla extract
1 cup semisweet chocolate chips
¾ cup walnuts, chopped
⅓ cup whole almonds

Preheat oven to 350 degrees. Line muffin pan with paper liners. In a medium bowl, sift together flour, cocoa, sugar, baking soda, baking powder, and salt. In a large bowl, stir milk, egg, oil, and vanilla. Mix dry ingredients into large bowl; beat well. Add chocolate chips and walnuts; stir well. Fill muffin cups ¾ full. Poke almonds into tops of unbaked muffins. Sprinkle muffins with sugar. Bake for 20 to 25 minutes or until toothpick inserted in center comes out clean.

Oatmeal Chocolate Chip Muffins

1¼ cups quick-cooking oats
1¼ cups milk
1 egg
½ cup vegetable oil
¾ cup brown sugar, packed and divided

¾ cup semisweet chocolate chips
1 cup pecans, chopped and divided
1¼ cups flour
4 teaspoons baking powder
1 teaspoon salt

Preheat oven to 400 degrees. In a medium bowl, combine oats and milk. Allow to stand for 15 minutes. Grease or line a muffin pan with paper liners. Stir egg, oil, ½ cup brown sugar, chocolate chips, and ½ cup pecans into the oat and milk mixture. In a large bowl, combine flour, baking powder, and salt. Add oat mixture to the flour mixture, stirring until just moist. Fill each muffin cup ⅔ full. Sprinkle tops with the remaining brown sugar and pecans. Bake for 20 to 25 minutes.

Chocolate Cinnamon Chip Muffins

2 cups all-purpose biscuit
   baking mix
⅓ cup sugar
2 tablespoons vegetable oil

1 egg, slightly beaten
½ cup cinnamon chips
½ cup semisweet chocolate chips
⅔ cup milk

Preheat oven to 400 degrees. Line muffin pan with paper liners. In a large bowl, combine baking mix, sugar, vegetable oil, egg, cinnamon chips, chocolate chips, and milk. Fill muffin cups ⅔ full. Bake 15 to 18 minutes or until golden brown.

Chocolate Apple Bread

1 cup and 2 teaspoons sugar,
   divided
3/4 teaspoon cinnamon, divided
3/4 cup walnuts, finely chopped and
   divided
2 cups flour
1/2 teaspoon salt
1/2 teaspoon baking powder
1/2 teaspoon baking soda

1/4 teaspoon nutmeg
1/2 cup butter, softened
2 eggs
1 teaspoon vanilla extract
2 tablespoons buttermilk
2 cup apples, peeled, cored, and
   coarsely chopped
1 cup semisweet chocolate chips

Preheat oven to 350 degrees. In a small bowl, combine 2 teaspoons sugar, 1/4 teaspoon cinnamon, and 1/4 cup walnuts; set aside. In a medium bowl, mix flour, salt, baking powder, baking soda, remaining cinnamon, and nutmeg; set aside. In a large bowl, cream butter and remaining sugar together; add eggs and vanilla. Gradually add the flour mixture and buttermilk. Fold in apples, remaining walnuts, and chocolate chips. Pour mixture into a greased 9x5 inch loaf pan. Sprinkle with the sugar, cinnamon, and walnut mixture. Bake for 55 to 60 minutes. Allow to cool for 20 minutes before removing from pan.

Chocolate Zucchini Bread

3 cups flour
¼ cup unsweetened cocoa powder
1 tablespoon ground cinnamon
1 teaspoon baking soda
½ teaspoon baking powder
1 teaspoon salt
2 cups sugar

3 eggs
1 cup vegetable oil
2 teaspoons vanilla extract
2 cups zucchini, shredded
1 cup walnuts, chopped
1 cup semisweet chocolate chips

Preheat oven to 350 degrees. Lightly grease two 9x5 inch loaf pans. In a large bowl, combine flour, cocoa, cinnamon, baking soda, baking powder, and salt; mix well. In a separate bowl, combine sugar and eggs, beat until well blended. Add oil and vanilla; beat until well combined. Stir in zucchini. Pour zucchini mixture into flour mixture and stir until just moistened. Stir in nuts and chocolate chips. Spoon evenly into prepared pans. Bake for 55 to 60 minutes or until toothpick inserted in center comes out clean. Allow to cool in pans for 10 minutes. Remove bread from pans and cool completely on wire racks.

Chocolate Chip Orange Zucchini Bread

3 cups flour
¼ teaspoon baking powder
1 teaspoon baking soda
1 teaspoon salt
½ teaspoon ground cinnamon
1 teaspoon ground nutmeg
3 eggs

2 cups sugar
1 cup vegetable oil
2 teaspoons vanilla extract
2 cups zucchini, grated
2 cups walnuts, chopped
1 cup semisweet chocolate chips
1 tablespoon orange zest

Preheat oven to 350 degrees. Grease two 9x5 inch loaf pans; set aside. Sift together flour, baking powder, baking soda, salt, cinnamon, and nutmeg. In a large bowl, beat eggs until light and fluffy. Add the sugar and continue beating until well blended. Stir in oil, vanilla, zucchini, nuts, chocolate chips, and orange zest. Blend in the sifted ingredients. Turn batter into the prepared pans. Bake for 50 minutes or until a knife inserted in the center comes out clean. Allow to cool completely before slicing.

Chocolate Chip Pumpkin Bread

3 cups sugar
1 (15 ounce) can pumpkin puree
1 cup vegetable oil
⅔ cup water
4 eggs
3½ cups flour
1 tablespoon ground cinnamon

1 tablespoon ground nutmeg
2 teaspoons baking soda
1½ teaspoons salt
1 cup mini semisweet chocolate
  chips
½ cup walnuts, chopped

Preheat oven to 350 degrees. Grease and flour three 9x5 inch loaf pans. In a large bowl, combine sugar, pumpkin, oil, water, and eggs; beat until smooth. Blend in flour, cinnamon, nutmeg, baking soda, and salt. Fold in chocolate chips and nuts. Fill loaf pans ¾ full. Bake for 1 hour or until a knife inserted in center comes out clean. Cool on wire racks before removing from pans.

Chocolate Banana Bread

1 cup butter, softened
2 cups sugar
4 eggs
6 bananas, mashed
2 teaspoons vanilla extract

3 cups flour
2 teaspoons baking soda
½ cup unsweetened cocoa powder
1 cup sour cream
1 cup semisweet chocolate chips

Preheat oven to 350 degrees. Lightly grease two 9x5 inch loaf pans. In a large bowl, cream together butter, sugar, and eggs. Stir in the bananas and vanilla. Sift in flour, baking soda, and cocoa; mix well. Blend in sour cream and chocolate chips. Pour the batter into the prepared pans. Bake for 55 to 60 minutes, or until a toothpick inserted in the center comes out clean.

And the angel said unto her,
Fear not, Mary:
for thou hast found favour with God.
And, behold, thou shalt conceive in thy womb,
and bring forth a son,
and shalt call his name Jesus.

LUKE 1:30–31